Side by Side:

A Model for Healthy Relationships

KATE ARMS

ISBN: 978-1-9994302-4-5

CONTENTS

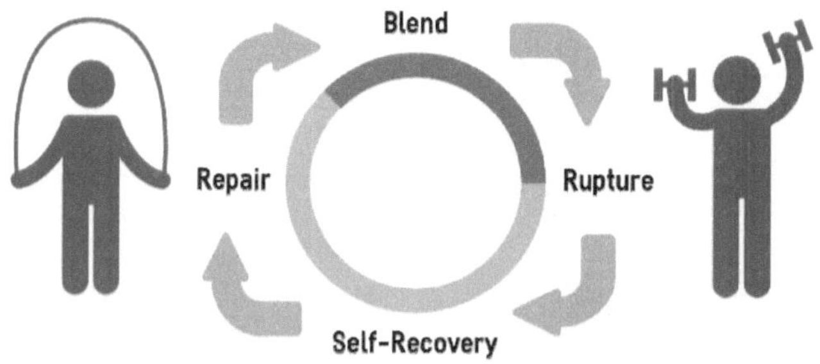

WHAT IS A HEALTHY RELATIONSHIP?

A healthy relationship is a relationship in which each participating member is thriving as an individual as the group works effectively together to meet relationship goals.

Different relationships have different goals. Business relationships serve business goals: productivity and profit. Healthy relationships at work create thriving businesses and motivated, productive, and engaged workers.

Personal relationships are typically focused on fun, mutual support, and a sense of belonging. Healthy relationships in friendship and love grow intimacy and self-actualization. Your relationships with the people you live with are about community and sharing the costs and labour associated with housing.

1

SIDE BY SIDE

WHAT MAKES A RELATIONSHIP HEALTHY?

Relationships between people are healthy when people bring their authentic selves into relationship.

Each person has their own story, their own self, and their own choices to make.

Each person is complete on their own and thrives when in alignment with their own inner wisdom.

A healthy relationship does not require any specific depth of connection. A connection can involve leaning on each other and providing mutual support to one another, walking beside each other, or doing separate things for some time.

What matters is that the individuals involved find what works for them.

Whatever the form of the relationship or the degree of interdependence, each person remains responsible for taking care of themselves. If people lean on each other without simultaneously remaining responsible for themselves, the unhealthy result is co-dependency.

Relationships go through a four-stage cycle: Blending, Rupture, Self-Recovery, and Repair.

A healthy relationship navigates through the stages on an ongoing basis, responding to changing needs and goals through each iteration of the cycle.

STAGE ONE: BLENDING

When two people meet, one initiates conversation, the other responds. If this connection develops further, each person takes turns leading with the other following their lead.

At first there is often a clear sense of who is driving the connection forward in any given moment.

As the relationship continues, the source of leadership may no longer be obvious. This is the Blended stage.

If this happens, the two are responding to each other with such engagement and subtlety that they seem to be acting as a single unit. The interactions between them feel easy and mutual to both individuals.

STAGE TWO: RUPTURE

The "honeymoon" phase that is fully Blended is temporary.

Inevitably, one person's needs and goals will steer them in a direction that the other person doesn't instinctively follow. The blended unit will dissolve again into two separate individuals.

After the Blended state ruptures, the individuals have to make a choice. They can separate completely and drop their connection, or they can recreate their connection in a new way.

For a healthy relationship to continue, both individuals have to go through a process of Self-Recovery and then lean into the Repair stage.

STAGE THREE: SELF-RECOVERY

In the Blended stage of relationship, people feel like who they are and what the relationship is asking of them are the same thing. The relationship feels natural and easy.

Once a Rupture occurs, however, they have to pay attention to their own needs and the needs of the relationship separately in order to make sure that they are not sacrificing too much of themselves for the other person or for the relationship.

This typically requires some time checking in with themselves and getting clear on their personal emotional state, desires, needs, and goals. Individuals may need time or privacy to do the work of Self-Recovery. This may feel like a lull in the relationship or a time of disconnection.

During Self-Recovery, each person takes care of their own needs, lifting their own weights as it were. If people try to do each other's work during this phase, they will bend themselves out of shape and may injure themselves.

The most important part of Self-Recovery is creating

space between the emotional disruption caused by the Rupture and a person's sense of choice about how to react.

After individuals have clarified their needs and goals, they must initiate Repair.

STAGE FOUR: REPAIR

Repair is the choice that both individuals make to find new ways of being connected to each other after a conflict or divergence.

The Repair process takes the relationship back through conscious leading and following to a new Blend. If the underlying connection is deep, Repair may be quick even after major Ruptures. At other times, it feels like a struggle to find a new harmony.

In a healthy relationship, a person who supports another does it by choice and has the capacity to make a different choice. In the Repair stage, people actively choose to stay connected despite the Rupture.

In all four stages of a healthy relationship, each person remains responsible for protecting their own values and integrity.

During Repair, it is particularly important that individuals express their needs to each other and do not attempt to support the other person in any way that requires sacrificing their own integrity or values. They must assume that the other person is competent and is taking responsibility for themselves.

For many people, the hardest part of maintaining healthy relationships is initiating Repair after a difficult Self- Recovery.

Even if no one is ever tired, hungry, sick, or cranky, there will be differences of opinion and conflicting authentic desires and values. Initiating Repair is a fundamental relationship skill.

NAVIGATING THE FOUR STAGES

For a healthy relationship to persist, the individuals must stay in relationship with each other through the Self-Recovery and Repair stages.

When Self-Recovery requires taking time apart, the Rupture may feel permanent to one or both individuals. It can be helpful to remind each other that this is a part of the process of being in relationship and not inevitably an ending.

Willingness of each person to show up authentically and with their whole self and to witness the other's whole self without judgment or agenda creates the environment for healthy relationships where both individuals can thrive.

Being present with and connected to another person requires allowing them to have an impact. Not only must you let people act in accordance with their own inner authority, you must accept it when they do.

The Repair process may lead to major changes in the relationship. Creating a relationship that is healthy for all the individuals involved requires being open to that possibility.

There will be ruptures, times of conflict. That is inevitable.

Healthy relationships manage conflict rather than being destroyed by it.

The four stages of the Side by Side model provide a framework for understanding how to create and maintain a healthy relationship despite conflicts.

SIDE BY SIDE MAY FEEL CHALLENGING

Western culture gives us mixed messages about independence. Child-rearing practices often push children to certain types of independence earlier than other cultures do. Our family and business cultures often involve stoic independence and self-reliance.

On the other hand, western notions of romantic love and passion-based marriages throughout popular culture include myths of lack and dependence. The myth that each person has one person who will complete them runs deep.

In the Side by Side Model, each person is considered a unique individual with the capacity to connect to their inner authority and the power to make choices in accordance with that wisdom. A healthy relationship in this model involves mutual choice of the appropriate level of interdependence.

WHAT ABOUT GROUPS, FAMILIES, OR TEAMS?

Things get more complicated in groups larger than a pair.

Each pair of people within the group has their own direct connection and the interlocking connections create a group body that has a dynamic of interactions that tends to exert pressure on individuals to conform.

In small groups, individuals create direct relationships with other people individually. As groups get larger, intentional shaping of structures by leaders becomes more important because those structures impact the relationships between individuals who have not connected directly with each other.

At its core, however, a group is made up of the relationships amongst its members.

If the individuals who make up the group engage in authentic relationships based on respect for each other's wisdom about their own lives, the group is likely to either naturally occur in forms that support individual thriving or to burst out of restrictive boundaries and reform in a healthier way.

HOW TO PUT THIS MODEL INTO ACTION

If you look at your relationships through the lens of this model, you will be able to see which stage of the model you are in. This will help you identify the moments of Rupture, which call for you to do your Self-Recovery work and make offers of Repair.

Seeing the cycle as a cycle provides a sense of perspective. A Rupture event does not mean that a relationship is bad or unhealthy or ending. It means that the work for the next period of time is on Self-Recovery and that will be followed by repairing the relationship.

This work is not always easy. Support yourself by gathering with others who approach the world this way and learning how to support each other.

At first, you will probably find yourself aware only of big Ruptures and Self-Recovery and Repair challenges that feel difficult. As you become more skilled, you will notice more subtle Ruptures that are more easily Repaired. These smaller course corrections generally reduce the likelihood of major Ruptures occurring in the future.

In addition, with practice, you will find that Self-Recovery and Repair become easier even in the wake of major Ruptures.

THE KEY TO REPAIR

The greatest gift that we can give another person is to stand in our own inner authority and actively look for the best things about them.

This non-judgmental, compassionate witnessing gives them space and permission to be their brightest selves.

When two people relate to each other in this way, the relationship brings out the best in both of them.

When people feel at their best and believe that they are talking to people who see the best in them, it is easier for them to engage in the work of redesigning relationships in the wake of Ruptures.

The healthiest thing individuals can do both for themselves and for the greater society is to embrace the assumption that every adult is competent, with powers of agency and wisdom about what is true for them.

LEARN MORE

For a deeper dive into the practical skills of using the model to improve your relationships, sign up for the Side by Side newsletter at www.signalfirecoaching.com and get the 32-page *Side by Side Guide to Hard Conversations* as a free gift.

ABOUT THE AUTHOR

Kate Arms, J.D., CPCC, PCC, is the founder of Signal Fire Coaching. She works with organizations and corporate leaders to create cultures where people are not only effective but happy. She also offers classes and private coaching to help smart, sensitive, and creative people harness their many passions and use that energy to thrive.

Her writing focuses on emotional, social and relationship intelligence and skills. She has written on healthy interpersonal relationships at home and work, how to have effective high-stakes conversations, managing emotional intensity, building resiliency, antifragility, and more.

She runs the *Thrive with Intensity* program and developed the Side by Side Model of Healthy Relationships.

Follow her online on Twitter (SignalFireKate), Facebook (KateArmsCoach), Instagram (SignalFireKate), and LinkedIn (KateArmsCoach).